# SIX FEET BACK, SATAN

## 4 Weeks in the Book of Ephesians

## Margaret Feinberg

D1607302

# Contents

Introduction ........................................................................................ 4

DAY 1 **Your Vast Arsenal in Christ** Ephesians 1:1 (NIV) ........................... 6

DAY 2 **Can You Snub God's Provision?** Ephesians 1:2-10 (NIV) ................ 7

DAY 3 **How to Overcome Purposelessness** Ephesians 1:11-14 (The Message) ........................................... 9

DAY 4 **Celebrate Your Wins** Ephesians 1:15-23 (NIV) ............................. 11

DAY 5 **Jaw-Dropping Before and After Pics** Ephesians 2:1-10 (NIV) ........ 13

DAY 6 **How to Send the Enemy Packing** Ephesians 2:11-22 (NASB) ........ 14

DAY 7 **The Unfolding Mystery of Christ** Ephesians 3:1-13 (NIV) ............. 16

DAY 8 **The One Thing You Need Today** Ephesians 3:14-21 (NASB) .......... 18

DAY 9 **How to Tap Into Exponential Power** Ephesians 4:1-6 (ESV) .......... 19

DAY 10 **When You're Facing an Infodemic** Ephesians 4:7-16 (NIV) .......... 21

DAY 11 **Don't Push the Wrong Button** Ephesians 4:17-24 (ESV) ............. 22

DAY 12 **How Footholds Become Strongholds** Ephesians 4:25-32 (NIV) .... 24

DAY 13 **The Scent of God and the God of Scent** Ephesians 5:1-2 (NIV) .... 25

DAY 14 **Never Give Your Affection to This** Ephesians 5:3-14 (HCSB) ....... 27

DAY 15 **How to Have Delightful Conversations** Ephesians 5:15-21 (NKJV) ........ 28

DAY 16 **We Must Nourish Love In Love** Ephesians 5:22-33 (NIV) ............ 30

DAY 17 **The Redemptive Work of God** Ephesians 6:1-9 (NIV) ................. 32

DAY 18 **The Quickest Way to Overcome the Enemy** Ephesians 6:10-12 (HCSB) ........ 34

DAY 19 **Your Pre-packed Battle Gear** Ephesians 6:13-17 (NKJV) ............ 35

DAY 20 **The Stupendous Power of Prayer** Ephesians 6:18-23 (HCSB) ....... 37

# Introduction

A few weeks ago, I collapsed from physical and emotional exhaustion. In the wake of a global pandemic and economic recession, my life veered off-road and I wandered into uncharted territory. My husband, Leif, was thrust into 70-hour work weeks pastoring our congregation. Six months of my speaking events were postponed or canceled. People we loved fell ill, and some died. An eight-hour work day now felt like fourteen, and quarantine left me feeling severed from society. I'd pushed and pivoted until my fatigued body screamed, "Enough!"

I climbed into bed for a nap—and slept for two and a half days.

Maybe you're feeling weary and longing for rest too. What once felt like a sprint now seems like an ultramarathon. The unending uncertainty continues to take a toll on your friendships, mental health, marriage, and your confused kiddos. Perhaps the virus scorched your wedding plans, graduation party, job promotion, income, or your dreams for 2020.

Maybe you're among the immunocompromised like me. Taking a simple step through your front door is now an activity fraught with fear. Lifelong friends now look like threats that you are forced to avoid, despite longing for their touch. Each new governmental strategy to safely reengage in life forces you to take carefully calculated risks, adding exhaustion to exhaustion.

The principles God offers us for flourishing in the midst of terrible oppression and difficulty are, thankfully, still alive and well and always will be. Even when the threat of the virus has disappeared, devastating side effects from the pandemic may linger or new challenges will creep in. Either way, if there's one principle I've learned in more than two decades of ministry, it's this: Whenever we encounter adversity, the adversary comes out to play.

We're all facing physical and emotional challenges during this time, but we're naïve to overlook the accompanying spiritual challenges. The adversary of God is known as the evil one, the devil, or *ha-satan* in Hebrew. This malicious entity appears in the book of Job asking God if he can test a faithful man through suffering, loss, and pain. All four Gospels recount stories of spiritual attack. Jesus faces off against God's adversary in the wilderness and wins, and on the cross, he defeats the destruction monger.

Even though the war has been won, the battle continues until Jesus' return.

Cartoons often depict the devil with horns and flame-red pitchfork, but Jesus describes "the father of lies" (John 8:44) as a swindler, assassin, and arsonist who schemes to burn everything to the ground. One of the adversary's chief aims is to distort the truth of who God is and who you're called to be. He hopes to derail your relationship with God and render you unfruitful.

The adversary represents everything that's against Christ and the Kingdom of God. Jesus came to deliver abundant life—more and better than you ever dreamed (John 10:10). God's blueprint for your life abounds in peace and patience, goodness and gentleness, joy and hope. God adorns you with grace, guards you through self-control, and surrounds you with boundless reservoirs of divine affection.

In this spiritual battle with the accuser, God counters by sending the Advocate. The Holy Spirit empowers us to overcome the enemy's lies and walk in God's provision and power—even during a global pandemic, even in seasons of uncertainty, even in times of suffering.

Penned from a prison cell, Paul's letter to the Ephesian church reorients our thinking. Our battle has never been against flesh and blood, he says, but against darkness and evil in all its forms. Ephesians unveils the depths of our spiritual blessings and illuminates God's marvelous plan to make us alive through Christ.

This study is designed to empower you to overcome the wily ways of the enemy. Through the power of the Holy Spirit, you'll be attuned and equipped so every time the accuser draws near, you'll declare, "Six feet back, Satan!" and send him back where he belongs.

Margaret

# Your Vast Arsenal in Christ

## I

¹ Paul, an apostle of Christ Jesus by God's will: to the faithful saints in Christ Jesus at Ephesus, the faithful in Christ Jesus:

If you've ever second-guessed whether the Bible remains relevant, look no further than Ephesians. This timeless writing speaks to humanity's deepest struggles and longings.

Theologian Frederick Buechner describes the apostle Paul's ministry this way: "Jesus exploded on the scene like a bomb and blew the world in general and the world of Judaism in particular sky-high. It was left to Paul to try to sort out the pieces."

A vehement opposer to the church, Paul had a spiritual encounter with Jesus that wiped the crust from his blind eyes and flipped his world right-side-up. He became a spiritual papa to churches throughout the Middle East, Europe, and parts of Asia.

When he finds himself in a Roman prison for making bold Jesus proclamations, he refuses to allow thick, dingy walls or rusty chains to hold him back. He pens letters to the beloved church he's been raising up.

The opening verse reveals the author, Paul, along with the recipients, believers in Ephesus. This wealthy port city was an ancient Greek city under Roman rule that boasted the famous temple of Artemis. Pilgrims still visit the ancient remains of the city today in modern-day Turkey.

If you enjoy a pinch of academic debatery, it's worth noting some early manuscripts don't mention "in Ephesus," leading some to believe that the letter was meant to be circulated among all churches.

You can divide the six-chapter book of Ephesians into halves like a two-act play. The first three chapters center on our purpose and identity in Christ. The final three address how we should live in light of these truths. The sharp transition between the two sections is difficult to miss: "As a prisoner for the Lord, then, I urge you to live a life worthy of the calling you have received" (Ephesians 4:1).

Like the culture Paul addresses, ours wrestles with divisiveness and polarization. (Have you watched any news lately?) Like Ephesus, we must live on high alert for every form of elitism, exceptionalism, and racism that creeps into our hearts. We need God and each other as much as ever before. Ephesians draws us together in divisive times by reminding us that we're hand-fashioned for belonging, connection, and unity. Without it, we cannot inhale, and even worse, we cannot exhale the Spirit within us.

When it comes to the enemy and spiritual warfare, it's tempting to read Ephesians waiting for the stockpile of battle armor in the final chapter. That's when we're told to gird up with the splendid six:

the belt of truth, breastplate of righteousness, boots of peace, shield of faith, helmet of salvation, and sword of scripture.

But what if Paul is equipping us with a vast arsenal throughout *all* the chapters of Ephesians? What if through Christ you're being made battle-ready with so much more? The enemy is wily, but God has made you wieldy. You can march forward radiating grace, practicing forgiveness, demonstrating sacrificial love.

You can scorch the enemy's plans through prayer and worship. You can demolish the enemy's lies by declaring your true identity in Christ. You can abolish the enemy's thievery by reciting your inheritance from God.

When the enemy tries to invade your space, you can thrust out your forward facing palm and declare, "Six feet back, Satan. I am Christ's, and he is mine."

1. How does knowing that Paul wrote this letter from a dank, dingy cell affect the way you read his words? Why does someone speaking life out of pain seem more impactful?

2. Read Acts 9:1-22. What does this passage reveal about Paul's transformation? What kinds of experiences have been the most transformational in your life?

3. When it comes to overcoming the wily ways of the enemy, what are your go-to tactics?

4. In what ways has Christ been making you holy and faithful (v. 1)?

# Can You Snub God's Provision?

# 2

## EPHESIANS 1:2-10 (NIV)

[2] Grace and peace to you from God our Father and the Lord Jesus Christ. [3] Praise be to the God and Father of our Lord Jesus Christ, who has blessed us in the heavenly realms with every spiritual blessing in Christ. [4] For he chose us in him before the creation of the world to be holy and blameless in his sight. In love [5] he predestined us for adoption to sonship through Jesus Christ, in accordance with his pleasure and will— [6] to the praise of his glorious grace, which he has freely given us in the One he loves. [7] In him we have redemption through his blood, the forgiveness of sins, in accordance with the riches of God's grace [8] that he lavished on us. With all wisdom and understanding, [9] he made known to us the mystery of his will according to his good pleasure, which he purposed in Christ, [10] to be put into effect when the times reach their fulfillment—to bring unity to all things in heaven and on earth under Christ.

"You should apply for unemployment."

I balked at our accountant's advice. I'd never applied for unemployment in my life and didn't think I'd qualify. He explained that with all speaking events canceled for the foreseeable future, a large chunk of my income was about to vanish. Under the new rules of the pandemic, this meant I qualified for unemployment benefits, which could help carry us through until we secured small business loans and future writing contracts.

As I considered and prayed about the decision, I sensed Holy Spirit whisper, "Why do you despise my provision?"

Ouch! My mind recalled the image of Jacob sprinkling in the final ingredients of his famous spicy stew. When his brother Esau arrives with a growling belly and begs for a taste, Jacob eyes the opportunity of a lifetime. He offers to trade a scoop of soup for his elder brother's birthright worth a double portion of the inheritance. It's not exactly a fair trade.

A few satisfying slurps later, Esau shrugs off the grand provision that comes with being a firstborn and despises his birthright (Genesis 25:34).

Much like Esau, I was snubbing God's provision. I only wanted God's provision if it arrived in familiar packaging, the same dimensions and shapes he'd used in the past. Though I claimed God as my provider, I despised the new wrappings of the provision.

We can turn our noses up to divine promises and provision. We can slap on a "return to sender" label through our attitudes and actions. When the Waymaker makes a way, we can foolishly shout, "No way!" and go our own way.

I followed the accountant's advice and thanked God for his provision, and more importantly, for revealing himself as my provider in the ways he sees fit.

Paul launches his letter to the church at Ephesus by opening our eyes to the bounty of God's promises and blessings. While the world says you can be filthy rich, God makes you flawlessly rich in everything money can't buy. You are lavished with every spiritual blessing. You're called, chosen, adopted, adored, renewed, and redeemed. You're flush with favor and forgiveness.

You're even given a destination, a holy destiny, that God has hand-selected with delight. Paul avows, "This is who you are. This is where you're headed. This is your birthright. In Christ, you have it all, all, all."

The enemy wants us to look down on our spiritual bounty and turn up our noses. He wants to convince you that you're a pauper begging for every crumb, unsure if it will come. That's when the accuser murmurs, "You're forgotten and neglected. God has abandoned you." We must silence that voice with the truths found in this passage.

So often we are able to celebrate the redemption in others' lives, but not our own. We accept that others are chosen or forgiven, but we can't believe the same for ourselves. Instead of living like God's prized possession, we sit in spiritual alleyways shaking tin cups and begging for blessings like despised outcasts.

The enemy's lies are always there for the taking, but you can thwart him. As you reread through today's passage, invite the Holy Spirit to search your heart for the spiritual bounty and blessings you've subtly snubbed or coolly dismissed. Then enter anew into the celebration of the riches of God's grace.

1. What unusual or unexpected ways has God provided for you during the pandemic?

2. Did you embrace his provision or turn up your nose to it? Explain.

3. Read Genesis 25:24-34. Why do you think Esau gave up his birthright? What tempts you most to give up your birthright as a child of God?

4. Which of the promises or blessings of God in Ephesians 1:2-10 do you need to cling to extra tight right now?

# How to Overcome Purposelessness

# 3

## EPHESIANS 1:11-14 (THE MESSAGE)

11-12 It's in Christ that we find out who we are and what we are living for. Long before we first heard of Christ and got our hopes up, he had his eye on us, had designs on us for glorious living, part of the overall purpose he is working out in everything and everyone.

13-14 It's in Christ that you, once you heard the truth and believed it (this Message of your salvation), found your-selves home free—signed, sealed, and delivered by the Holy Spirit. This signet from God is the first installment on what's coming, a reminder that we'll get everything God has planned for us, a praising and glorious life.

Shortly after the pandemic struck America, many of my friends and I wrestled with purposelessness. Fulfilling jobs and ministries were suddenly snatched away from so many of us. We were once certain God had given us those assignments for kingdom purposes, but we now felt unsure. New tasks for which we weren't trained were thrust on us (homeschooling, anyone?) and left us feeling exhausted. Meanwhile, those with too much time were left feeling useless.

Extroverts and caregivers were separated from those they poured their lives into, and they felt impo-tent. Introverts were quarantined with others and now lacked privacy. They struggled to find solitude for the work and hobbies that once helped them flourish.

Businesses that took a lifetime to build shuttered. Beloved employees were laid off. Families were devastated.

Amid increasing job insecurity, health challenges, financial pressures, and friends falling sick and passing away, many of us felt the thick fog of sadness descend. If there's one atmosphere the en-emy loves, it's gloom. In the thick haze of heaviness and the mire of murkiness, he can lead us to believe that our prized and precious lives lack purpose.

Christ has been eyeing you since the beginning of time, laying a rich blueprint for your good and his glory. In Christ alone you discover who you are and what you're living for!

Being stuck in quarantine during a pandemic had a winnowing effect. Many things I once clung to for meaning and purpose vanished in a blink. All the events on our social calendar were crossed off one by one—from my weekly dinner club with friends in Utah to our annual vacation with other friends from across the country. Each time the phone rang, I winced from the expectation that it was another event coordinator calling to cancel. My productivity dipped, and my perfectionism was no longer sustainable. I believed that Christ was the anchor of my purpose, but it felt like my life was somehow becoming less meaningful.

"My purpose is in Christ alone," I whispered..

What's amazing is that God has given you everything you need to do everything he has called you to do. When you decided to follow Jesus, God placed his insignia on you. You were sealed with the Holy Spirit.

When Paul penned his letter to the Ephesians, those who read it would have been familiar with this process. In antiquity, a signet ring was pressed into wax or clay to create a seal on something with private or critically important contents. The Romans often sealed the edges of their parchment communications or decrees to ensure no one could tamper with them undetected. In the same way, you have been sealed by God, and no enemy or force can tamper with the contents of who you are and your God-given purpose.

While the enemy wants you to live in a fog about your future, God invites you to discover your divine purpose. Simply pray, "Holy Spirit, what do you want me to do today?" Then sit and wait and listen. Pay attention to thoughts that come to mind. If Spirit gives you small steps to take, you can trust they're significant.

A word of encouragement seems insignificant … unless you're deep in depression.
A card sent by snail mail seems insignificant … unless you're immunocompromised and feeling isolated.
A small grocery store gift card seems insignificant … unless you just got laid off and don't have a cushion in your savings account.

Just follow Spirit's nudges and let God sort out the impact. With every act of obedience, you'll discover purpose in your life and send the enemy and his lies packing.

Some days as you ask the Holy Spirit how to order your day, you may hear him say, "I just want to be with you." That's a powerful reminder that the most important thing you can do *for* God is simply be *with* him. When you lean into the Holy Spirit, you'll discover more than your purpose; you'll find the one in whom you live and move and find your being now and forever (Acts 17:28).

1. Do you think the question "What's your purpose?" is more of a man-made question or a divine question? Explain.

2. In what area of your life have you wrestled with purposelessness?

3. How would you describe your purpose in life? Do you feel like you're fulfilling your purpose? Why or why not?

4. In what ways have you pursued Jesus to find out who you are what you're living for (v. 11)? What has been the result?

## Celebrate Your Wins

## 4

### EPHESIANS 1:15-23 (NIV)

[15] For this reason, ever since I heard about your faith in the Lord Jesus and your love for all God's people, [16] I have not stopped giving thanks for you, remembering you in my prayers. [17] I keep asking that the God of our Lord Jesus Christ, the glorious Father, may give you the Spirit of wisdom and revelation, so that you may know him better.

[18] I pray that the eyes of your heart may be enlightened in order that you may know the hope to which he has called you, the riches of his glorious inheritance in his holy people, [19] and his incomparably great power for us who believe. That power is the same as the mighty strength [20] he exerted when he raised Christ from the dead and seated him at his right hand in the heavenly realms, [21] far above all rule and authority, power and dominion, and every name that is invoked, not only in the present age but also in the one to come.

[22] And God placed all things under his feet and appointed him to be head over everything for the church, [23] which is his body, the fullness of him who fills everything in every way.

Shortly after quarantine began, a flurry of memes and posts on Instagram warned that if I didn't learn a new skill or language or musical instrument or accomplish a big project, then I had wasted this time.

My friends became overnight schoolteachers for their kiddos, worked double-time for companies struggling to stay afloat, and did their best to show love to their spouses, parents, neighbors, co-workers, and other friends. If they squeezed in a shower and a tray of tater tots for their kids, they deserved a gold medal and 10,000 points.

If you found time to learn to play the guitar or repaint your house, well done. Personally, I am awarding myself a gold medal and 10,000 points because I could still put on the same pair of jeans after quarantine. Granted, they didn't zip or button, but I still got them on.

Looking back at this nagging, low-grade sense of discouragement that lingered over so many people, I recognize two of the enemy's favorite tools: guilt and shame.

My friend Nathan confessed he felt like a failure because he hadn't learned French or completed any significant projects during this season. I replied, "I think you're an overcomer." I listed out all I saw. How he'd grown more sensitive to God and the Holy Spirit during this time. How he'd made wise decisions for his health, stayed safe, and practiced good mental hygiene. He'd trimmed his budget and inspired others through social media. Sure, he hadn't completed a new project, but he'd planned one out. In my mind, I said, he's winning.

"Well, when you say it like that!" Nathan responded with a laugh.

Sometimes we need our friends to help us celebrate our wins. We need others to give us perspective and speak life and hope into us. That's what Paul does for the church of Ephesus. He doesn't just pray for his friends, he reminds them who they are in Christ, and reorients them to their heavenly perspective. Revelation 4 describes God's throne room bedazzled with radiant jewels and lustrous gold. Peals of thunder and flashes of lightning backdrop the mysterious creatures who echo, "Holy, holy, holy is the Lord God Almighty, who was, and is, and is to come" (Revelation 4:8).

The scene reveals God as all-sovereign, all-powerful, all-holy, no matter the heartache or heartbreak, the discouragement or disease, the pickle or predicament we face. All are right-sized when we place ourselves in awe and worship at the foot of the throne.

That's why Paul prays "that your heart may be enlightened in order that you may know the hope to which he has called you, the riches of his glorious inheritance in his holy people, and his incomparably great power for us who believe" (vv. 18-19).

Sometimes we can become so distracted by everyday life that we need to raise our eyes toward the throne room to regain a hope-filled, heavenly view—for our sake and for others'.

Who do you know who's experienced discouragement and hopelessness at the enemy's hands? Who desperately needs words of affirmation? Your choice words can shut the mouth of the enemy and infuse courage. In speaking life and hope into others, you'll often discover it for yourself. Don't delay, reach out today.

1. What's one of your wins that you can celebrate from the last few months? How did Christ empower and equip you for that win?

2. What attributes of God are most meaningful to you right now? (All-powerful, all-present etc.)

3. Read Revelation 4. What stands out to you from this chapter? What does it mean for you to have a throne-room perspective?

4. Who are three people you can celebrate with your words today?

# Jaw-Dropping Before and After Pics

# 5

[1] As for you, you were dead in your transgressions and sins, [2] in which you used to live when you followed the ways of this world and of the ruler of the kingdom of the air, the spirit who is now at work in those who are disobedient. [3] All of us also lived among them at one time, gratifying the cravings of our flesh and following its desires and thoughts. Like the rest, we were by nature deserving of wrath.

[4] But because of his great love for us, God, who is rich in mercy, [5] made us alive with Christ even when we were dead in transgressions—it is by grace you have been saved. [6] And God raised us up with Christ and seated us with him in the heavenly realms in Christ Jesus, [7] in order that in the coming ages he might show the incomparable riches of his grace, expressed in his kindness to us in Christ Jesus.

[8] For it is by grace you have been saved, through faith—and this is not from yourselves, it is the gift of God— [9] not by works, so that no one can boast. [10] For we are God's handiwork, created in Christ Jesus to do good works, which God prepared in advance for us to do.

Have you ever started a new eating regimen and snapped before and after photos?

As self-confessed foodies, Leif and I have engaged in quite a few diets together. To inspire us to continue eating well, we'll often start by snapping photos from the front, back, and sides. Then every few weeks we take new photos to encourage us that our lifestyle changes are paying off.

In today's passage, the apostle Paul provides jaw-dropping before andr after photos of our spiritual lives. This is a then and now look at what happens when you surrender to the rule and reign of Christ. These revealing snapshots are more than Instagram-worthy:

You once were spiritually dead.
Now you're spiritually flourishing.

You once lived entangled by sin.
Now you're free to fulfill the good works God has prepared for you.

You once drifted in the current of the world under the dark ruler.
Now you're raised, aligned, and seated with Christ in the heavenly realm.

You once lived by fleshly desires.
Now you live in union with Christ.

You once were under the wrath of God.
Now God's gracious hand and favor rest on you.

You once lived by striving.
Now you're rescued by grace.

You once boasted in what you could do.
Now you boast in what God can do.

Look at the breathtaking portraits of your salvation. Through Christ, God now has you exactly where he wants you. Each day you get to join the work that God's already doing. This is God's great big gift from beginning to end.

The question for you today is what snapshot have you been paying more attention to, the before or the after?

Perhaps you're tempted by the accuser to allow your weaknesses and mistakes to take center stage. Maybe you still cringe from memories of past mistakes and poor choices. Or maybe that one misstatement keeps buzzing through your brain despite asking for forgiveness and pursuing reconciliation.

Remember: It's from these and more that you have been saved. You are not a before in Christ, you are an after in Christ. You are a stunning display of God's salvation, and don't let anyone—especially the enemy—tell you otherwise.

1. In what ways do you focus too much time or attention on your life before Christ?

2. What memories from the past is the accuser using to weigh you down with discouragement? How can you fight back using Ephesians 2:1-10?

3. Above, where this portion of Scripture is written, circle all the words that imply before and after. For example, consider "used to live" (v.2). Now notice which phrases are used repeatedly. How does this repetition underscore the main idea of this passage?

4. Take a moment to personalize the before and after of your life in Christ. Make a list of what your life was like (in non-religious terms) before Jesus, as well as after. Take time to give God thanks for the good work he's started and promises to complete in you.

# How to Send the Enemy Packing

# 6

**EPHESIANS 2:11-22 (NASB)**

[11] Therefore remember that formerly you, the Gentiles in the flesh, who are called "Uncircumcision" by the so-called "Circumcision," *which is* performed in the flesh by human hands— [12] *remember* that you were at that time

separate from Christ, excluded from the commonwealth of Israel, and strangers to the covenants of promise, having no hope and without God in the world.

[13] But now in Christ Jesus you who formerly were far off have been brought near by the blood of Christ. [14] For He Himself is our peace, who made both *groups into* one and broke down the barrier of the dividing wall, [15] by abolishing in His flesh the enmity, *which is* the Law of commandments *contained* in ordinances, so that in Himself He might make the two into one new man, *thus* establishing peace, [16] and might reconcile them both in one body to God through the cross, by it having put to death the enmity.

[17] And He came and preached peace to you who were far away, and peace to those who were near; [18] for through Him we both have our access in one Spirit to the Father. [19] So then you are no longer strangers and aliens, but you are fellow citizens with the saints, and are of God's household, [20] having been built on the foundation of the apostles and prophets, Christ Jesus Himself being the corner *stone*, [21] in whom the whole building, being fitted together, is growing into a holy temple in the Lord, [22] in whom you also are being built together into a dwelling of God in the Spirit.

We moved so many times as a child. With every new school and state, I wrestled with the question, "Do I belong?"

My eyes became laser-focused on those who showed any kindness, those who remembered my name, those who invited me to join them for lunch or a sleepover. Decades later, I still walk into new places with that same question ringing in my ears. I suspect most of us do. We all long to belong.

This deep human longing for belonging is the source of Paul's next before and after comparison. Before Christ, we were outsiders, foreigners to God's people, unable to access the fullness of the promises, provision, and presence of God. Paul uses the word "uncircumcised" for those who had not received the mark of the covenant like Abraham had received (Genesis 17:10-14). "Uncircumcised" refers to all of us before Christ.

We were separate and strangers. We did not belong. Now, through Christ, we've been brought into the warm embrace of God's affection. He demolished the barricade between us and himself. Jesus became our peace, our shalom, so that we would bring God's peace everywhere we go.

The Greek word for peace, *eirene,* appears eight times here in Ephesians and almost 50 times throughout all Paul's letters.

Our God is a God of *eirene* (Romans 15:33).
Christ is the prince of *eirene* (2 Thess. 3:16).
The good news is a gospel of *eirene* (Ephesians 5:16).
The Spirit ushers us into a life of *eirene* (Romans 8:6).
The kingdom of God is marked by *eirene* (Romans 5:1).
The goal of our relationships is *eirene* (Ephesians 4:3).
"Peace, peace, peace," Paul shouts.

The Person of Peace, Christ, came to abolish separation, defeat suspicion, and bring unity. The arms of the Christ and the arms of the cross welcome you no matter what you've done or where you've been. You're no longer a floater or foreigner, an outsider or the odd one out. You're now fitted together brick by brick with all of God's children with Christ as the cornerstone.

That's why the adversary tries to tear us apart. The enemy works double-time against love, against grace, against justice. He wants us to become competitive and critical, to overlook and oppress, to diminish and discredit.

We must be on high alert for divisiveness. That means we can no longer look on another human who is a reflection of God and say, "I resent or reject you for that."

God is still constructing "a holy temple built by God, all of us built into it, a temple in which God is quite at home" (Eph. 2:22, MSG). This holy place of belonging won't be complete without you—and those who differ from you.

1. Which believers have you judged, criticized, or alienated because their perspective on politics or the pandemic is different from yours? Have others judged, criticized, or alienated you?

2. Why do you think the enemy is thrilled when we construct barriers between ourselves and other believers?

3. When we devalue those who are different, what is the dark fruit of that division?

4. How can you allow the love and peace of Christ to reign in those relationships where you're struggling?

# The Unfolding Mystery of Christ

# 7

## EPHESIANS 3:1-13 (NIV)

[1] For this reason I, Paul, the prisoner of Christ Jesus for the sake of you Gentiles—

[2] Surely you have heard about the administration of God's grace that was given to me for you, [3] that is, the mystery made known to me by revelation, as I have already written briefly. [4] In reading this, then, you will be able to understand my insight into the mystery of Christ, [5] which was not made known to people in other generations as it has now been revealed by the Spirit to God's holy apostles and prophets. [6] This mystery is that through the gospel the Gentiles are heirs together with Israel, members together of one body, and sharers together in the promise in Christ Jesus.

[7] I became a servant of this gospel by the gift of God's grace given me through the working of his power. [8] Although I am less than the least of all the Lord's people, this grace was given me: to preach to the Gentiles the boundless riches of Christ, [9] and to make plain to everyone the administration of this mystery, which for ages past was kept

hidden in God, who created all things. [10] His intent was that now, through the church, the manifold wisdom of God should be made known to the rulers and authorities in the heavenly realms, [11] according to his eternal purpose that he accomplished in Christ Jesus our Lord. [12] In him and through faith in him we may approach God with freedom and confidence. [13] I ask you, therefore, not to be discouraged because of my sufferings for you, which are your glory.

Do you notice a word that keeps re-appearing in today's reading?

No? Ok. Here's a hint: This word appears four times, and many of us have a love-hate relationship with it. Yep, now you see it!

Like Paul, I love the word "mystery." Well, not the word itself, but what "mystery" represents. I love a good mystery with sophisticated sleuths, persistent cops, and a surprise plot twist. Throw in a private eye, some fiery car chases, and a double agent, and I'll binge for sure. Mysteries stimulate our intellects as we pay extra attention to the details and clues. They spark our imagination for becoming a hero and bringing justice to this world.

But most of us don't want *everything* to be a mystery. In real life, we tend to prefer concrete to ever-shifting sands, the known to the unknown. When it comes to planning a day or scheduling a meeting, consistent and quantifiable come in handy.

The Greek word for mystery is *mystírio,* meaning a secret of God that can be revealed only by God. In today's passage, Paul calls the gospel, or good news, of Jesus "a mystery"—but one that's been revealed. He has received insight into this mystery as the Holy Spirit has worked in his life alongside other church leaders (v. 5), and he assures us we have access to the shame knowledge (vv. 2-3).

In Ephesians 6:19, he writes, "Pray also for me, that whenever I speak, words may be given me so that I will fearlessly make known the mystery of the gospel." This mystery is ever unfolding, revealing new depths of Christ and bringing both Jewish and Gentile people together to feast at a table of grace.

While Paul knows God's marvelous ultimate plan for all who are in Christ, he doesn't know every detail of his own earthly life. Remember that Paul pens this letter from prison. He's followed the Spirit through emotional blows and physical beatings, storms and shipwrecks. He knows firsthand what it means to be deserted and downcast.

Most of us don't want God or his plans for our lives to be like a game of "Clue." We want it to resemble an easy-to-follow driving app with a British narrator who politely tells us which way to turn. We want God to mark a clear route home when we find ourselves off the beaten path. And when we feel totally lost, like, say, in the middle of a pandemic, we want that British narrator to calmly reassure us that life will soon return to its previous state.

Alas, following Jesus doesn't eliminate the mysteries of life. Rather it unveils the depths of Christ in our mysterious situations. Like Paul, we may not know when our suffering will end or what tomorrow's news will bring. But we can hold this unknowing in one hand while grasping in the other a confident assurance that we are intimately known by God.

Rest assured, the God who has seen you through your past will carry you to your God-given future.

1. In what area of your life are you most struggling to trust God with the unknown?

2. When you're facing the unknown or a mystery in life, which do you tend to pray for more: information or transformation? Explain.

3. If Jesus is an unfolding mystery, how can you become more intentional about knowing him more intimately?

4. Look up Romans 16:25-26, Ephesians 1:9-10, and Colossians 1:25-27. What does each passage reveal about the mystery of the gospel?

# The One Thing You Need Today

# 8

## EPHESIANS 3:14-21 (NASB)

[14] For this reason I bow my knees before the Father, [15] from whom every family in heaven and on earth derives its name, [16] that He would grant you, according to the riches of His glory, to be strengthened with power through His Spirit in the inner man, [17] so that Christ may dwell in your hearts through faith; *and* that you, being rooted and grounded in love, [18] may be able to comprehend with all the saints what is the breadth and length and height and depth, [19] and to know the love of Christ which surpasses knowledge, that you may be filled up to all the fullness of God.

[20] Now to Him who is able to do far more abundantly beyond all that we ask or think, according to the power that works within us, [21] to Him *be* the glory in the church and in Christ Jesus to all generations forever and ever. Amen.

On a recent episode of *The Joycast* podcast, a wise man named Jack Deere told me, "People go their whole Christian life and never understand that Jesus wants to be friends with them."

Deere highlighted John 15:15, in which Jesus tells the disciples they're no longer called servants, but friends. "The essence of friendship isn't about service, though we'll serve our best friend in a heartbeat," Deere said. "We're best friends with someone because of the pleasure we have when we're with them and because of the way we feel loved by them."

Jesus wants to take us beyond duty and obligation to an experience rooted in pleasure. The Son of God wants us to feel his affection and how much he loves us.

"That's the biggest lack in the church," Deere said. "Most people say, 'I know God loves me,' but not very many people feel the love of God."

I suspect the enemy celebrates every time he can distract and pull us away from experiencing divine affection. If he can convince us that we can't feel God's love, then he'll try to convince us that God's love should be questioned … then doubted … then dismissed altogether.

The conversation with Jack challenged me to begin pursuing the affection of God through prayer. In today's reading, we discover what and how to pray. Paul bows his knees, centering himself on the reality of the throne room, and asks the Holy Spirit to strengthen us through supernatural power in the reality of God's love. Though I'd read of the width, length, height, depth, and mysterious dimensions of God's affections many times before, I now saw this passage is a prayer—a petition we can make on our own behalf and for others. I prayed:

*Father, through the power of your Spirit, help me explore the lengths, trek the widths, ascend the heights, and probe the depths of your love. Today, Lord, I want to sense your divine affection. Amen.*

Nothing noticeable happened that first day. But over time, I found the posture of my life shifting as I became more attentive to God's postcards of love. A gentle presence. The calm in the midst of anxiety. Passages of love rising off the pages of scripture. Now they weren't for someone else, they were for me. Over time, I found myself living more wide-eyed and open-hearted to the sweetness of his presence. And I pray the same for you.

*Father, help us to experience the fullness of your love each and every day. Amen.*

1. When was the last time you felt the affection of God? Describe the experience.

2. Read 1 John 3:1, Zephaniah 3:17, and Isaiah 54:10. What does each passage reveal about the transforming power of God's love? Why is experiencing God's love so important to your spiritual life?

3. Why do you think you don't experience the affection of God more often? What would it look like to create more space in your life to intentionally pursue God's affection?

4. How can you make Ephesians 3:16-19 your own personal prayer? Write a version of this passage in your own words.

# How to Tap Into Exponential Power

# 9

EPHESIANS 4:1-6 (ESV)

[1] I therefore, a prisoner for the Lord, urge you to walk in a manner worthy of the calling to which you have been called, [2] with all humility and gentleness, with patience, bearing with one another in love, [3] eager to maintain the unity of the Spirit in the bond of peace. [4] There is one body and one Spirit—just as you were called to the one hope that belongs to your call— [5] one Lord, one faith, one baptism, [6] one God and Father of all, who is over all and through all and in all.

On the night of his arrest, Jesus could have asked his Father for anything—extreme wealth, abundant safety, or prestigious positions. He doesn't ask for any of these.

Jesus prays that all his followers may be one. "Just as you, Father, are in me, and I in you, that they also may be in us, so that the world may believe that you have sent me" (John 17:21). The sacred relationship between Father, Son, and Spirit is interlaced in unity, and we are called to emulate the divine collective.

In Ephesians, Paul echoes Christ's call to unity. In a single sentence, he uses the word "one" seven times—"one body, one Spirit, one Lord, one hope, one faith, one baptism, one God." In a culture mired in polarization and division, the heart cry of Christ remains that we would be united.

The enemy despises unity, because he knows its secret power; when believers come together, there's exponential power. Ecclesiastes 4:12 teaches that though one can be overpowered, two can defend themselves, and a cord of three strands is not quickly broken. This is more than basic addition.

Leviticus 26:8 demonstrates this principle, too: "Five of you will chase a hundred, and a hundred of you will chase ten thousand, and your enemies will fall by the sword before you." In kingdom mathematics, the unity of five increases power by twenty times, the unity of a hundred incrases power by one hundred times. Though it doesn't make any earthly, logical sense, it demonstrates the powerful multiplication factor of oneness.

When the accuser keeps us at odds with each other, the odds are in his favor. But God's favor rests on us when we come together. As any military commander can tell you, an army must maintain a "unified front" if it hopes to defeat the enemy.

We must live on high alert for those interactions that pull us apart. Sometimes it's the misspoken words, the harsh tone, the broken promise. We can hurt others by what we do or leave undone. Paul encourages us not to wait, but to become eager beavers in restoring relationships.

When it comes to reconciliation, Paul challenges us to gird ourselves with humility. Humility may not seem like a top-tier, go-to strategy, but removing any granules of pride softens us so we can receive feedback and trust God with the process. Alongside humility, we must exude gentleness, which can alter the atmosphere of any conversation. Coupled with patience, we can carry each other forward in love and live in unity.

1. Who are you at odds with or suspicious of right now? How has your response differed from what Paul instructs in Ephesians 4:2-3? What can you do to reconcile and create unity?

2. Describe a time when you've experienced the exponential power of unity. Why does Jesus long for us to be one?

3. Read Romans 12:16, Philippians 2:1-4, and Colossians 3:3-14. What does each passage reveal about the purpose and power of unity?

4. Who are three people you can reach out to today to strengthen your friendship with them?

# When You're Facing an Infodemic

# 10

[7] But to each one of us grace has been given as Christ apportioned it. [8] This is why it says: "When he ascended on high, he took many captives and gave gifts to his people." [9] (What does "he ascended" mean except that he also descended to the lower, earthly regions? [10] He who descended is the very one who ascended higher than all the heavens, in order to fill the whole universe.) [11] So Christ himself gave the apostles, the prophets, the evangelists, the pastors and teachers, [12] to equip his people for works of service, so that the body of Christ may be built up [13] until we all reach unity in the faith and in the knowledge of the Son of God and become mature, attaining to the whole measure of the fullness of Christ. [14] Then we will no longer be infants, tossed back and forth by the waves, and blown here and there by every wind of teaching and by the cunning and craftiness of people in their deceitful scheming. [15] Instead, speaking the truth in love, we will grow to become in every respect the mature body of him who is the head, that is, Christ. [16] From him the whole body, joined and held together by every supporting ligament, grows and builds itself up in love, as each part does its work.

One my biggest frustrations in the early days of the virus was conflicting reports. It became increasingly difficult, sometimes impossible, to identify and understand the truth. The pandemic has been nicknamed an "infodemic" because of the lack of factual information and overabundance of misinformation. I latched onto a particular theory early on. When I shared my perspective with others, they refuted it, yet I insisted on being right.

A pastor friend sat me down and had a crucial conversation. He challenged me to examine the scientific reports, triangulate my news sources, and wait on casting judgment with the ever-changing developments.

"Remember that people don't need to hear a theory about the virus as much as they need to hear and see the reality of Christ in you," he said.

Turns out my pastor friend was right. The theory I had clung to was soon debunked, and in some ways, my witness had been too. I had peddled misinformation and wasted valuable time and energy spreading distrust rather than infusing others with hope and faith.

For me, the conspiracy theory provided a sense of control and security in a constantly changing situation. But the last thing my little corner of the world needed was me running around and crying wolf about a serious issue. I asked my friends to forgive me and placed a new filter on my conversations with loved ones: *Does it help others grow into the fullness of Christ?*

In today's passage, Paul reminds us that on the cross Jesus conquered death and darkness. Jesus descends to us that we might ascend with him—not just at the end of life but in our every day.

We need people around us—leaders, prophets, evangelists, shepherds, teachers, family, and friends—to have healthy crucial conversations when we become distracted. We must stop ourselves and ask, "How can I use my words to build others up into all they're called to be in this season?" "What do I need to do to exhale the hope and life of Christ everywhere I go?" "Are my conversations centered more on the crisis or on the work of Christ?"

When the discussion veers toward the polarizing and hazardous, we can rise above and redirect our words toward that which is good and true and beautiful.

1. Margaret confesses clinging to a conspiracy theory because it gave her a sense of control. Why do people often cling to conspiracy theories? Outside of the coronavirus crisis, have you ever clung to a conspiracy theory? If so, describe. How did that theory make you feel better about yourself or the situation?

2. What stories have you been telling yourself or others that have really been vehicles for spreading fear?

3. What do 1 Peter 3:10, Colossians 4:6, and Proverbs 21:23 reveal about the importance of what we speak and share with others?

4. What are three questions you can use to refocus a conversation toward that which is good and true and beautiful when the discussion is becoming tense?

# Don't Push the Wrong Button

# 11

**EPHESIANS 4:17-24 (ESV)**

[17] Now this I say and testify in the Lord, that you must no longer walk as the Gentiles do, in the futility of their minds. [18] They are darkened in their understanding, alienated from the life of God because of the ignorance that is in them, due to their hardness of heart. [19] They have become callous and have given themselves up to sensuality, greedy to practice every kind of impurity. [20] But that is not the way you learned Christ!— [21] assuming that you have heard about him and were taught in him, as the truth is in Jesus, [22] to put off your old self, which belongs to your former manner of life and is corrupt through deceitful desires, [23] and to be renewed in the spirit of your minds, [24] and to put on the new self, created after the likeness of God in true righteousness and holiness.

Have you ever stood in an elevator pressing the "Close Door" button multiple times in hopes of moving quicker? Yeah, me too. But what if I told you those buttons don't actually do anything?

Well, they don't.

Pressing "Close Door" won't make the doors shut faster. Why? Because when the Americans with Disabilities Act of 1990 passed, it required that doors remain open long enough for someone with a mobility issue to board safely. It's an ineffective button.

How about this one: Have you ever stood at a crosswalk rapidly clicking the button to make the light change? Well, a recent study found that of the 1,000 crosswalks in New York City, pressing the button affects the timing of the light change on fewer than 100 of them. The buttons provided a service to pedestrians, until over time they interfered with the coordination of traffic as the number of vehicles on the road skyrocketed. And this isn't just true of The Big Apple; you'll find it in Boston, Dallas, Seattle, and other cities across the country. [1]

Why would a city retain an ineffective button? In addition to the cost of removing or updating older installations, placebo buttons are kept to give us the illusion of control because they have a net-positive effect of making us feel better.

Sin is a lot like those crazy buttons that seem to be broken. Sin gives us the illusion of control all the while maintaining control over us. We tell ourselves that we'll get away with sin, and no one will know. We assure ourselves that we deserve this particular pleasure at this particular time and that it won't be particularly costly. We reassure ourselves that we could stop if we really wanted to. But sin creates a cycle of broken promises.

Paul reminds us that standing on the street corner of life and pressing the button of sin is no way to live. That kind of life only leads to a jaded heart filled with greed and grime. The life of Christ is so much more! He empowers us to pitch our old way of living and slip on a life of freedom.

The Hebrew word *shalom* encompasses the ideas of wellbeing, satisfaction, and wholeness in God. My friend Troy Champ observes, "Whether we call it shalom or not, it's the goal of every human being. We chase it through a variety of different ways. Whether you realize it or not, you're reaching for shalom every time you reach for sin." [2]

Perhaps during the pandemic you've dealt with loneliness through some less-than-savory means, and now you find yourself trapped in a zoo of lust or self-sabotaging behaviors. Or when your city started reopening, you found yourself judging those spooky people who drew different boundaries than you. Or maybe you've found yourself sliding toward some dark addiction in order to cope.

Instead of pressing the button of sin, we can press into a fulfilling relationship with God. Sin has an allure, for sure. But remember that in all the Lord asks, he has only our good in mind. In aligning ourselves with Christ, we discover fullness in our work, relationships, and the abundant life.

1. Why are you feeling the urge to push the button of sin right now? What strategies have you enacted to help you overcome the temptation?

2. When you look back over the last month, when have you chased after peace but acted on your desire through sin? What was the result?

3. How do Romans 6:4 and Romans 7:6 underscore Paul's declaration in Ephesians 4:20-24?

4. In your own words, how have you become a new creation in Christ (see 2 Corinthians 5:17)? What grimy clothes of your old life have you tossed in the dumpster? Which are you still clinging to?

# How Footholds Become Strongholds

# 12

EPHESIANS 4:25-32 (NIV)

[25] Therefore each of you must put off falsehood and speak truthfully to your neighbor, for we are all members of one body. [26] "In your anger do not sin": Do not let the sun go down while you are still angry, [27] and do not give the devil a foothold. [28] Anyone who has been stealing must steal no longer, but must work, doing something useful with their own hands, that they may have something to share with those in need.

[29] Do not let any unwholesome talk come out of your mouths, but only what is helpful for building others up according to their needs, that it may benefit those who listen. [30] And do not grieve the Holy Spirit of God, with whom you were sealed for the day of redemption. [31] Get rid of all bitterness, rage and anger, brawling and slander, along with every form of malice. [32] Be kind and compassionate to one another, forgiving each other, just as in Christ God forgave you.

Some people blame Satan for every misplaced hair. Couldn't find their favorite granola in the grocery store? It was the enemy's fault. Missed a deadline at work? The devil made them do it. A belly ache after eating too many BBQ ribs? It had the evil one's fingerprints all over it. Satan can become an excuse to shirk personal responsibility and the one to blame for every imperfection.

Others give Satan too little credit. For them, the enemy is little more than a mythic figure or the source of entertainment in popular movies and shows. The idea that there's a supernatural force in opposition to God with actual power in this world sounds Stone Age. Laughable even.

C.S. Lewis warned, "There are two equal and opposite errors into which our race can fall about the devils. One is to disbelieve in their existence. The other is to believe, and to feel an excessive and unhealthy interest in them. They themselves are equally pleased by both errors, and hail a materialist or a magician with the same delight." [3]

Paul mentions the work of the enemy throughout Ephesians. In today's passage, he provides a striking detail regarding the work of the adversary. Anger is a healthy and God-given emotion. We are designed to feel angry when we encounter injustice. Anger helps us know our boundaries. But it can lead us toward sin if we allow it to simmer and explode thoughtlessly.

I experienced this after a friend's betrayal. I burned with rage. As the extent of what he'd done became more apparent and the devastation from his actions grew, I felt an Incredible Hulk rage overtake me. Every time I thought of him, I fumed. Soon I began hoping awful things would happen to him. In nurturing the furor, I crossed the line into hatred.

In the process, I gave the enemy a foothold. I agreed with the lies of the accuser. I went from condemning this person's acts as bad to condemning my friend as a *bad person*. In bitterness, my mind echoed a chorus of harshness. Whenever someone mentioned the person's name, I rushed to tell my side of the story, which slipped into slander. Months later, the mere thought of the person sent me into an emotional spiral.

That's when I realized the unforgiveness in my heart invited the enemy in. What began as a foothold transformed into a stronghold. Breaking free required me to break the agreements I'd made with the accuser--agreements such as "he's a bad person" and "he's irredeemable." I needed to forgive, to let go, to bless the person who wronged me. I wish it happened overnight, but it took me months of prayerful persistence and asking the Holy Spirit's help to do what I could not do on my own.

To overcome the wily work of the adversary, Peter calls us to spiritual attentiveness. First Peter 5:8 says, "Be alert and of sober mind. Your enemy the devil prowls around like a roaring lion looking for someone to devour."

Rage provides a foothold, and the remaining verses highlight other opportunities for the enemy to slip a toe in the door—thievery, violent self-assertion, and malicious speech. Yet we can rise above.

Every time we respond with kindness and compassion, we're shouting, "Six feet back, Satan!" The Holy Spirit guides us through all of this, empowering us to overcome every attack of the enemy.

1. Describe a time when you became so upset about something, you couldn't sleep or you said something you later regretted. How did the accuser operate to steal your peace and harm your relationships?

2. What overwhelming emotion have you allowed the devil to use as a foothold in your life? What negative or harsh thoughts toward someone are festering in your life right now?

3. Who do you need to forgive and show compassion and kindness to in order to break free from the work of the accuser? How will you act on this today?

4. Paul makes it clear we can choose to give the enemy a place in our lives, or we can choose to walk in step with the Spirit. How will you become more attentive and obedient to God's Spirit today?

# The Scent of God and the God of Scent

# 13

## EPHESIANS 5:1-2 (NIV)

[1] Therefore, be imitators of God, as dearly loved children. [2] And walk in love, as the Messiah also loved us and gave Himself for us, a sacrificial and fragrant offering to God.

When I traveled to Paris with a friend several years ago, we rented a tiny apartment through Airbnb. The unit matched the description minus one detail: the residence perched above a chocolatier.

Each morning, we opened the windows and breathed in chocolaty sweetness. Throughout the days, we visited museums, scouted for the city's best croissant, and people-watched from cafes. But the wafting scent of the chocolatier's magical creations remains my most vivid memory.

We all have memories marked by fragrances. The perfume that stirs memories of a loved one. The flower that triggers a childhood flashback. The waft of cookies that transport you back to Grandma's kitchen. God designed our brains so the olfactory system links to the same part of the brain that's associated with memory and emotions. That's why a long-forgotten scent stirs up images of the past and may even bring us to tears.

A study at Rockefeller University found that humans recall 1% of what they touch, 2% of what they hear, 5% of what they see, and 35% of what they smell. We remember about 200 different colors versus 10,000 different smells.[4]

The Bible speaks often of the olfactory nature of God. In Genesis 8, after the waters receded, Noah and his family emerged from the ark and roasted the meat of sacrificed animals as a burnt offering. God "smelled the pleasing aroma" (Genesis 8:21). This soothing odor calmed and delighted the Lord. God's inhale of grilled sacrifices appears more than three dozen times throughout the Old Testament.

God further instructed his priests to make incense offerings in the temple. In the Book of Revelation, we discover the golden bowls full of incense, which are the prayers of the saints (Revelation 5:8). God, who sees and hears all things, also has a nose that knows.

When Jesus exhaled the final breath of his fragrant life, the Father received it as a pleasing aroma. Paul calls us to be imitators of Christ—not just in word and deed, but in scent too. To the church in Corinth, Paul describes, "For we are to God the fragrance of Christ among those who are being saved and among those who are perishing" (2 Corinthians 2:15).

Author Lauren Winner points out that Paul could have described us as the light of Christ or the voice of Christ, but he handpicks fragrance. Winner observes, "Smell is an apt metaphor for Paul to use, precisely because smell can convey the presence of something that is far away. I smell bread baking the minute I walk through my front door, even though the source—the loaf in the oven—is in the kitchen; the smell tells me the loaf is there somewhere."[5]

In Ephesians 5, Paul calls us to be "imitators of God" who was himself the ultimate sacrificial and fragrant offering. Rather than run away from suffering and the cross, we are to be those who make a beeline for it. We are to approach with healing elements—oil and wine in hand—to bandage fallen sojourners' wounds, to provide transportation, safe housing, and long-term care.

We are to be those who practice mercy, fight for justice, and refuse to remain bystanders to the broken systems of this world. The fragrance of Christ rises in us not when we stay whole but when we're broken open and poured out in our love of others.

1. What's your all-time favorite smell? Least favorite smell? What memories do these invoke?

2. What's the fragrance of your life like right now?

3. Where do you most need to experience the sweet aroma of Christ's sacrifice and forgiveness?

4. Who is one person you can be broken open and poured out for today?

# Never Give Your Affection to This

# 14

[3] But sexual immorality and any impurity or greed should not even be heard of among you, as is proper for saints. [4] Coarse and foolish talking or crude joking are not suitable, but rather giving thanks. [5] For know and recognize this: Every sexually immoral or impure or greedy person, who is an idolater, does not have an inheritance in the kingdom of the Messiah and of God.

[6] Let no one deceive you with empty arguments, for God's wrath is coming on the disobedient because of these things. [7] Therefore, do not become their partners. [8] For you were once darkness, but now you are light in the Lord. Walk as children of light— [9] for the fruit of the light results in all goodness, righteousness, and truth— [10] discerning what is pleasing to the Lord. [11] Don't participate in the fruitless works of darkness, but instead expose them. [12] For it is shameful even to mention what is done by them in secret. [13] Everything exposed by the light is made clear, [14] for what makes everything clear is light. Therefore it is said: Get up, sleeper, and rise up from the dead, and the Messiah will shine on you.

When Moses panted his way to the crest of Mount Sinai, I doubt he knew he'd descend with the two most valuable slabs of stone in human history: ten commandments etched in rock. More than a rulebook, they offered Israel golden keys to how life works best.

*Nine:* Always tell the truth because your words are a rich treasury never to be spent frivolously.

*Six:* No matter how stompin' mad you get, never steal a life, because life belongs to God.

*Five:* Honor your parents even when it's hard. Though you didn't pick them, they can help you discover the story that grounds your life.

*Three:* God's name is holy and intimate, so don't toss it around so lightly. Even if you stub your nail with your hammer.

*Two:* Don't place your hope in trinkets and logos and magic formulas. Those shiny statues and emblems will ask you to bend a knee with your money or time or attention. Remember that God maintains a zero-tolerance policy toward idols—even those difficult to spot.

*One:* No matter how much other gods promise, never make room for any of them. God is jealous for your whole affection. Besides, other gods can't do anything for you anyway. Flash back to who rained down hail, split the Red Sea, and rescued you from Egypt. The Lord your God deserves every inch of your heart.

Those tablets are like twin love letters—gifts to know how best to live with God and alongside each other. In today's passage, Paul draws on the first of the commands when he challenges us to search our hearts for any form of idolatry within us. Idolatry stirs images of bending a knee to a golden statue (the second command), but worshiping something other than God begins in the inward places long before it finds an outward expression.

God gives us something as beautiful as love, but if we don't keep a watchful eye, we can grasp for alternatives to fill our deepest longings and needs. A lust for pleasure can lead to sexual promiscuity. A lust for power can lead to filthy practices. A lust for possessions can lead to greed. A lust for prattle can lead to gossip. A lust for popularity can fuel off-colored humor.

Lust is the pulse of idolatry, because it drives us to finding our satisfaction in anything other than God. That's why Paul challenges us to break ties with anyone who walks us down that dead daisy path. Step out of the darkness, he cries, and stroll in the radiance of God.

1. Reflecting on this passage, what are three idols that you've bowed your knee to in this season of life? Take time to ask God to free you from them.

2. In what area of your life are you lusting most right now? How will you find your satisfaction in God?

3. How have you seen God's commands leading you to the best possible life?

4. What's your greatest joy in being a child of God?

# How to Have Delightful Conversations

# 15

**EPHESIANS 5:15-21 (NKJV)**

[15] See then that you walk circumspectly, not as fools but as wise, [16] redeeming the time, because the days are evil.

[17] Therefore do not be unwise, but understand what the will of the Lord is. [18] And do not be drunk with wine, in which is dissipation; but be filled with the Spirit, [19] speaking to one another in psalms and hymns and spiritual

songs, singing and making melody in your heart to the Lord, [20] giving thanks always for all things to God the Father in the name of our Lord Jesus Christ, [21] submitting to one another in the fear of God.

"What's new with you?" Matt asked.

In the past I'd been able to offer a lively response to our long-time friend. I'd describe a new project or share a funny travel story. Now I felt trapped in a loop where each new day mirrored the last. It's hard to be a remarkable conversationalist when a trip to the grocery store or climbing out of jammies by 4 PM marks the highlight of your day.

I offered an awkward, blank stare as my brain scouted for a-n-y-t-h-i-n-g to say. I finally mumbled a new recipe that I hoped to try soon. *When in doubt, always talk about food.*

Life-giving conversation feels impossible when you're drained, overwhelmed, or worn out. In today's passage, Paul reminds us that it's exactly when we're feeling this way that the words we speak matter most. In days marked by discord and darkness, we must pay extra close attention to our spiritual lives. As we ask the Holy Spirit to infuse and empower us each day, we can speak words of life to others.

Notice the specificity in Paul's instructions: "Speak to one another in psalms and hymns and spiritual songs" (vs. 19). The Psalms are filled with honesty and heartache, confession and contemplation, lament and longing. They challenge us to bring our true selves to God and others. Through confession, our pain and suffering are thwarted by declarations of God's goodness. The Psalms remind us of the importance of vulnerability and authenticity with God and each other.

Hymns and spiritual songs speak truths that empower and inspire us. Their easily memorized, melodious lyrics ground us in the reliability of God. Great is his faithfulness even when the world feels out of control. When we see the stars and hear the rolling thunder, we see his power throughout the universe displayed. Because he lives, we can face tomorrow, no matter how uncertain it seems today. When we're soiled with sin, we remember that he makes beautiful things out of dust, and we rediscover the amazing grace that saves wretches like us.

Gratitude underscores these melodies of vulnerability, authenticity, and faithfulness. Even as we mourn what has been lost of late—including the lives we once knew—we can still discover pockets of thanksgiving.

How do you create delightful conversations? Enter your next interaction with two to three life-giving topics such as:

+What have been some of your wins during this season?

+What have you discovered about yourself in the past few months that you really like?

+Tell me about what you're reading, watching, or making.

+What's one thing you've really grown to appreciate?

+What song fires you up right now?

+Which of God's promises have meant the most to you recently?

Then follow up by asking for more details. Instead of allowing conversations to spiral downward, create upward spirals that lift hearts—including yours.

1. Why do you think it's important to come prepped with a few great questions when you're entering a conversation?

2. What's one go-to question you will use to create life-giving conversations?

3. What do Proverbs 18:21, Colossians 4:6, and James 1:19 reveal about the power of the words we speak and how to speak well?

4. Reflecting on the six conversation-sparking questions Margaret suggests, how would you answer each one?

# We Must Nourish Love In Love

# 16

## EPHESIANS 5:22-33 (NIV)

[22] Wives, submit to your own husbands as to the Lord, [23] for the husband is the head of the wife as Christ is the head of the church. He is the Savior of the body. [24] Now as the church submits to Christ, so wives are to submit to their husbands in everything. [25] Husbands, love your wives, just as Christ loved the church and gave Himself for her [26] to make her holy, cleansing her with the washing of water by the word. [27] He did this to present the church to Himself in splendor, without spot or wrinkle or anything like that, but holy and blameless. [28] In the same way, husbands are to love their wives as their own bodies. He who loves his wife loves himself. [29] For no one ever hates his own flesh but provides and cares for it, just as Christ does for the church, [30] since we are members of His body.[31] For this reason a man will leave his father and mother and be joined to his wife, and the two will become one flesh.

[32] This mystery is profound, but I am talking about Christ and the church. [33] To sum up, each one of you is to love his wife as himself, and the wife is to respect her husband.

Sixteen years of marriage to Leif have awakened my mind and being to new experiences, encounters, and viewpoints. They have enlarged me as an individual. For all the good worked in and through me so far, don't think for a moment that this mysterious holy union can be done well while napping. Year after year, decade after decade, we're still discovering what it means to live life together well.

Since our wedding day, I've become increasingly convinced the true beauty of marriage will never be found in the latest sex article in *Cosmo* or that lacy box of waxy chocolates on Valentine's Day. Those are cheap substitutes for real marriage: the day-to-day humble act of two people committed to life together no matter what tomorrow brings.

Paul reminds us that marriage is more than two people coming together; it's a holy mystery that provides a prism of Christ's love for the church. Some women read the word "submit" (v. 22) and bristle. They cease reading and miss the rest of this delightful passage. Paul calls women to submit to a man so head-over-heels in love with her and so surrendered to Jesus that he'll give up everything, even his life, for her. Paul never issues an authoritarian command or permit for men to be abusive or harsh. Rather, he calls husbands to a higher standard: to love their wives even when it costs them everything.

When it comes to loving each other, sometimes this is easier said than done. Some days marriage feels like a long catnap, nestled next to a window where the sun's rays warm my soul. Other days marriage feels like a tender embrace whispering, "You're not alone." And some days marriage feels like we're being pulled apart like an artichoke as we wrestle through fears, insecurities, miscommunication, and conflict.

In those moments of pain and strain, Paul challenges us to rise above the blame-and-shame game. When we can't see our partner clearly and accurately, we must raise our eyes to heaven for help. *Christ, how do I love when I don't have the faintest whiff of affection in me? How do I lay down my life and become more like you?*

Sometimes we must fight for our marriages through psychotherapy and pastoral care. Other times we must fight to spark sexual and emotional connection. In still other moments, we must learn to accept that though the other person does not change (and, ahem, we don't usually either), we can love them through Christ right where they are.

Paul calls all of us to nourish love in all its forms. It's not always easy. Statistics tell us that much. The passion we have for one another was never meant to have an expiration date.

1. In what ways does the marriage union reflect Christ and the church?

2. What's one way God is calling you to sacrificial love for your spouse or best friend? What causes you to hold back?

3. Read 1 Corinthians 13. How does this passage challenge and equip you to fulfill today's reading, whether to a spouse or a best friend?

4. What does it look like for you to madly love your friends?

# The Redemptive Work of God

# 17

[1] Children, obey your parents in the Lord, for this is right. [2] "Honor your father and mother"—which is the first commandment with a promise— [3] "so that it may go well with you and that you may enjoy long life on the earth."

[4] Fathers, do not exasperate your children; instead, bring them up in the training and instruction of the Lord.

[5] Slaves, obey your earthly masters with respect and fear, and with sincerity of heart, just as you would obey Christ. [6] Obey them not only to win their favor when their eye is on you, but as slaves of Christ, doing the will of God from your heart. [7] Serve wholeheartedly, as if you were serving the Lord, not people, [8] because you know that the Lord will reward each one for whatever good they do, whether they are slave or free.

[9] And masters, treat your slaves in the same way. Do not threaten them, since you know that he who is both their Master and yours is in heaven, and there is no favoritism with him.

To 21st century readers, Paul's words feel problematic and dangerous. After all, Southern white Americans interpreted passages like this to justify slavery and vilify the Underground Railroad. But if you dig into the original language and ancient culture, you'll find Paul's words subversive and revolutionary.

Paul addresses children first. In antiquity, females were considered less valuable than males. Instead of being educated, girls were assigned to chores and household duties. But the Greek word Paul uses for "children" is gender-neutral. He doesn't write to the male-centered culture of his time; he writes to all children.

As for parenting, fathers maintained absolute control and legal rights over their children. They decided whether a newborn would live or die. Baby girls could be abandoned or sold into slavery. Some dads used their authority to exercise harsh, abusive, and violent behavior.

Within this culture Paul calls children to practice obedience and honor their parents, an echo of the fifth commandment (Exodus 20:12). And he calls fathers to a higher standard too, one that doesn't permit abuse of any kind. The word "exasperate" means to spark anger. Rather than place unjust burdens on their children, dads must center their efforts on raising godly kids.

Paul then addresses the horrific evil of slavery. Scholars note that in the Greco-Roman world, slavery differed from the chattel slavery in early American history. It's estimated that one-third or more of those in Greece and the Roman Empire were slaves. People of every race and age were sold into slavery, taken captive during war, used to repay debts, or generally utilized simply to improve one's quality of life. Many were mistreated and abused, while others received respectable work such as household and business management. Male slaves often received training and education, and most gained freedom eventually. Jewish law actually forbid permanent slavery (Exodus 21:2-11),[6] though we shouldn't tolerate such an institution even for a day.

Now, some owners of slaves in Bible times viewed harshness and physical abuse as acceptable and even needed. Paul writes subversively, using a clever play on words. In antiquity, subordinates were not addressed; only privileged superiors were spoken to directly. Paul recognizes the slaves as members of God's family and addresses them directly in his letter, emphasizing their importance. He is lifting them up, offering them the dignity of their humanity. Something that others withheld.

Then he suggests something provocative: though they have earthly masters, their ultimate master is God. Paul's wordplay between "masters" and "their Master" suggests that slaves had a higher authority above their owners, just as the masters now had a higher responsibility to treat all people, including those in the slave class, with kindness and respect.[7] The idea of making slaves and their masters mutually submissive was a necessary and revolutionary leap toward equality. The Apostle presses the boundaries of the system and opens the door for future progress.

This isn't the only time Paul speaks against slavery. Paul writes to Philemon on behalf of Onesimus, a runaway slave. Paul urges the slaveowner Philemon to free Onesimus and offers, that if Onesimus owes anything then it should be charged to Paul's account (Philemon 1:18).

Unfortunately, this passage in Ephesians has been used to condone and perpetuate slavery and racism in countries around the world—including our own. The redemptive work of God calls us to eliminate slavery and fight for improved work conditions, better wages, and respectful and unified purpose between all levels within an organizational structure.

If we allow, these Scriptures challenge us to take a fresh look at the systems and institutions of our day and discover where we are contributing toward harm or oppression of others. They challenge us to become listeners and learners. Where is God challenging you to treat others differently? Spend your money differently? Live differently? Where can you join the redemptive work of God? All so others may experience the fullness of God's love and freedom in their lives.

1. Who has treated you harshly? How did that person make you feel? What will you do with those feelings?

2. Have you ever treated someone in a harsh manner because you felt the "right" to do so due to your position of authority? How will you humble yourself and make the relationship right?

3. What system or institution is contributing to the harm or oppression of others? How can you bring the kingdom of God into that situation?

4. What's one thing you will do today to honor and love your parents, even if they've passed?

# The Quickest Way to Overcome the Enemy

# 18

EPHESIANS 6:10-12 (HCSB)

[10] Finally, be strengthened by the Lord and by His vast strength. [11] Put on the full armor of God so that you can stand against the tactics of the Devil. [12] For our battle is not against flesh and blood, but against the rulers, against the authorities, against the world powers of this darkness, against the spiritual forces of evil in the heavens.

Who in your life wants you to fail? An ex-spouse? A coworker gunning for your job? A boss who has it out for you? A feuding neighbor?

When someone stands against us, we do everything we can to guard ourselves and win. In today's passage, Paul tells us of the real force that opposes us—and especially the Christ in us. God scripts a bright hope and future for us; while the adversary plots our spiritual demise. The most powerful word tucked into this passage is a single syllable and only three letters: *our*. That tiny word is easy to skip, but it's a key to victory.

"For *our* battle" (v.12) means that no matter what opposition comes along, we do not face it alone. Christ walks with us and before us strengthening us every step of the way. In the wilderness, Jesus taught that we can overcome the wily temptations of the adversary. Through the cross, Jesus stomped on death. In our spiritual battles, we are not alone because Christ is with us, with fellow believers marching alongside.

According to 1 Peter 5:9, we are to resist the prowling enemy and stand "firm in the faith, because you know that the family of believers throughout the world is undergoing the same kind of sufferings."

The enemy wants us to believe that we're all alone in our spiritual struggles. When we are isolated, we are easier to distract. And when we are distracted, we are easier to defeat. Yet you are never alone. Let me say it again. You are never alone.

Jesus intercedes for you. Fellow believers await to rally around you in prayer. And God has given you everything you need to stand strong. When it comes to spiritual warfare, one powerful principle I've discovered is:

The quickest way to make Satan small is to make God big.

When you're facing spiritual darkness, shine a spotlight on God. Lift up his name in prayer. Sing of his faithfulness. Declare his goodness aloud. Pen words of gratitude for his many blessings. Gather with others to break bread. Memorize powerful passages. Practice radical generosity. With every word and compassionate act, you'll send the enemy stumbling back where he belongs.

1. Where in your life have you sensed spiritual attack? How have you responded?

2. How will you develop friendships with those who can rally around you when you sense the work of the enemy? Do you call on them, or are you slow to do so out of privacy, pride, or timidity? Who can you rally around when they're facing spiritual attack?

3. What's one tactic the enemy has used recently against you? How have you overcome it?

4. What's one way you will make God big in your life today?

# Your Pre-packed Battle Gear

# 19

## EPHESIANS 6:13-17 (NKJV)

13 Therefore take up the whole armor of God, that you may be able to withstand in the evil day, and having done all, to stand. 14 Stand therefore, having girded your waist with truth, having put on the breastplate of righteousness, 15 and having shod your feet with the preparation of the gospel of peace; 16 above all, taking the shield of faith with which you will be able to quench all the fiery darts of the wicked one. 17 And take the helmet of salvation, and the sword of the Spirit, which is the word of God.

I have a pesky habit when traveling—namely, I tend to forget items at home. I'm not talking minor goods like a set of earbuds or a matching sock. Nope. I fail to pack the big-ticket items like underwear and makeup and shoes, which tends to cause awkwardness when you have to stand in front of other people and talk.

I arrived at an event once and—I kid you not—realized that I'd failed to pack pants. Worse yet, the location was so remote, there wasn't a clothing store within 50 miles. Now I like to travel in comfy clothes, but the baggy grey sweatpants I'd worn on the plane didn't exactly match any of my tops. I needed to be on stage within the hour, so the event organizer jumped on the radio and announced the predicament to every leader and volunteer.

"Could anyone loan the speaker a pair of pants?" she yelled before arching her head my direction. "Wait, what's your size?" I whispered her a number that women typically keep private just before she turned back to the radio and informed everyone.

The moral of the story? When you take a trip, pack your entire outfit and leave nothing behind. No stranger to traveling himself, Paul offers the same advice: put on the whole armor of God, every last piece and part.

Unlike my spotty packing practices, God pre-packs the battle gear for us. This "armor of God" is worn by God and issued to us as believers (Isaiah 11:5, 52:7, 59:17). The pieces—including truth, righteousness, readiness, faith, salvation and the gospel—require us to find our identity in Christ, to discover the characteristics of God manifest in us.[8]

In English, Paul appears to speak to individuals, but in the Greek, he's addressing the collective of believers as the church. When we collectively put on the armor of God, we become a mighty army of God.

Roman foot soldiers wore the protective covering mentioned. On the battlefield, each soldier tied a belt in the form of a leather apron-like covering around his midsections to protect vital organs. Breastplates guarded both the front and back of the soldier. Soldiers wore half-boots made of leather with studded soles and strapped to the ankles. This prevented slippage during long journeys and gave them a solid stance. The infantry used large shields estimated to be four feet tall and two to three feet wide, made of stretched leather covering a wooden frame, and reinforced with metal around the edges. When soaked in water, these shields quenched any flaming arrows. Helmets, often made of bronze, held a hinged visor. Swords defeated enemies on the battlefield.

Though God pre-packs our bags with this armor, we still have the responsibility to put the pieces on each day.

| | | |
|---|---|---|
| Belt | = | Truth |
| Breastplate | = | Righteousness |
| Boots | = | Peace |
| Shield | = | Faith |
| Helmet | = | Salvation |
| Sword | = | Word of God |

Notice the final piece of weaponry, the sword of the Spirit, differs in description from the previous ones. In the first five pieces, the second descriptive element defines the first: "belt of truth" or "breastplate of righteousness."But the "sword of the Spirit" is the "word of God." Also notice the first five pieces of armor are defensive, while the sword is an offensive instrument, through which God's power is displayed.

God gives you everything you need to overcome the adversary. As Eugene Peterson renders this text in The Message, "Be prepared. You're up against far more than you can handle on your own. Take all the help you can get, every weapon God issues, so that when it's all over but the shouting you'll still be on your feet. Truth, righteousness, peace, faith, and salvation are more than words. Learn how to apply them. You'll need them throughout your life. God's Word is an indispensable weapon" (Ephesians 6:13-17).

God calls us to be strong, alert, and ready just as he is strong, alert, and ready, on our behalf. He's pre-packed our spiritual bags, and we must now be intentional about putting all of it on. Not just some or most, but every last piece. When we do, we'll be ready for whatever the enemy brings.

1. Which piece of the armor of God are you quickest to put on each day? Which are you most likely to forget or overlook? Explain.

2. Which pieces of armor have you found most helpful in fighting your battles? Which have you found least helpful? Explain.

3. How many times does Paul emphasize standing in this passage? Why do you think he places such an emphasis on it? What does it look like for you to stand in the battles of life?

4. In a practical way, what does it look like for you to put on the armor of God each day?

# The Stupendous Power of Prayer

# 20

## EPHESIANS 6:18-23 (HCSB)

[18] Pray at all times in the Spirit with every prayer and request, and stay alert in this with all perseverance and intercession for all the saints. [19] Pray also for me, that the message may be given to me when I open my mouth to make known with boldness the mystery of the gospel. [20] For this I am an ambassador in chains. Pray that I might be bold enough in Him to speak as I should.

[21] Tychicus, our dearly loved brother and faithful servant in the Lord, will tell you all the news about me so that you may be informed. [22] I am sending him to you for this very reason, to let you know how we are and to encourage your hearts.

[23] Peace to the brothers, and love with faith, from God the Father and the Lord Jesus Christ. [24] Grace be with all who have undying love for our Lord Jesus Christ.

Prayer is an invitation, a request, and a command all tied into one mysterious spiritual activity that involves listening and learning, speaking and stillness, humility and hopefulness. Through prayer, we present parts of ourselves no one else sees to a God who already knows.

Yet listening to God has never come easy for me. Even after a morning of studying the scripture, an afternoon of engaging in life-changing conversation, or an evening absorbing soul-stirring teaching, there always comes a moment when self-doubt leaves me wondering, *God, was that really you? Was that your whisper or my own?*

With unsure footing, I'm learning that instead of listening for the whisper, I cup my ears and wait for the echo—those moments when God speaks the same message to my heart again and again.

Just as God invites us to be persistent in prayer, God is persistent with us. His words linger in our lives. Throughout conversations, daily life and study, the same idea or phrase or words will keep reappearing until I can no longer avoid their presence. God uses the repetitive nature of life and circumstance to get my attention, to familiarize me with his voice, to prepare my heart for what he wants to say.

If prayer is the sacred echo of our hearts communing with God, then the echo reverberates both ways. The sacred echo is not just our heartcry to God, but his heartcry to us.

No wonder Paul encourages us to pray at all times even over the most minute details. If we bring every teensy issue to God, then we won't hesitate when it comes to the big ones.

We are encouraged to pray in community just as we live in sacrificial love for one another. Though Paul asks for nothing since he began his letter, he now makes a request. Notice that he doesn't ask for a food delivery, financial support, or a show of gratitude. Rather, he asks for prayer.

Paul describes himself as an "ambassador in chains." In antiquity, an ambassador served as a legal representative of the emperor, often sent with an important message. During celebratory gatherings, ambassadors wore fancy chains as a symbol of the nations they represented. The word "chain" suggests a play on words. Though he's in imprisoned in a cell with chains, Paul's identity rests in the dignity of his work as God's servant.[9]

Sometimes I wonder how long Paul wrestled with God in prayer before he saw his situation from this perspective. It's oft said that prayer doesn't change God, it changes us. Ephesians, written from a dingy prison cell, embodies this truth in remarkable ways. Rest assured, every time you slather yourself and others in prayer, the enemy knows it's time to take at least six steps back.

1. How have you seen your prayer life grow and change over the last year?

2. Do you tend to bring God the details of life or only the biggies? Why?

3. What prevents you from having more ongoing conversations with God? How will you overcome those obstacles?

4. Who are three people you can reach out to today and offer to pray on their behalf?

## Endnotes

1   https://www.cnn.com/style/article/placebo-buttons-design/index.html
2   "Entangled" sermon by Troy Champ. Taught at Capital Church, January 18-19, 2020,
3   C.S. Lewis. *The Screwtape Letters*, HarperSanFrancisco, ©1942, Harper edition 2001, p. ix. 3
4   https://www.tailormadefragrance.com/en_us/blog/olfactive-memory/
5   Lauren Winner. *Wearing God: Clothing, Laughter, Fire, and Other Overlooked Ways of Meeting God.* HarperOne, 2015, p. 79.
6   We wince at the idea of a slave serving with "respect and fear," but it's important to remember this is common language for Paul. In 1 Corinthians 2:3, he uses the phrase to describe his own posture and approach when coming to visit the believers in Corinth. In 2 Corinthians 7:15, the same words are used to describe how the church responds to Titus. The phrase suggests a humble yielding in a relationship, not anxiety or dread.
7   Snodgrass, Klyne. *Ephesians: The NIV Application Commentary.* Zondervan, 1996, p. 321-323
8   Snodgrass, Klyne. *Ephesians: The NIV Application Commentary.* Zondervan, 1996, p. 339.
9   Barth, Markus. *Ephesians: The Anchor Bible.* Garden City: Doubleday, 1974. 2:782.

# Additional Lovelies
# Just for You

### Beautiful Life: 40 Days in the Book of James

The book of James overflows with doable and down-to-earth teaching on what it looks like to be a radiant follower of Jesus every day. You'll learn how to stand strong in the face of adversity, unleash the power of prayer, and live the true good life.

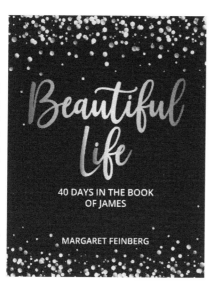

### Speak Life + Joy Greeting Cards

These modern, bright, and beautiful cards empower you to speak life and joy into those who need it most. Fun, colorful designs you can send to those you love. Five different designs available!

### Taste and See Book + Bible Study

Discover fishermen in the Galilee, bring in an olive harvest in Croatia, pluck figs in California and have the Bible come alive like never before.

### More Power To You

This 52-week devotional will help you overcome negative thoughts, break free from fear, and take your life back. The 90-second daily challenge will change the way you see yourself, God, and the world.

Visit margaretfeinbergstore.com to find fresh Bible studies, Speak Life + Joy greeting cards, and Scripture-based coloring books.

Made in the USA
Columbia, SC
09 October 2022

68914748R00024